PORTRAIT OF A LIFEBOAT HERO

Henry Freeman as rarely seen on photographs, relaxed and bare-headed. (Whitby Literary & Philosophical Society.)

PORTRAIT OF A LIFEBOAT HERO

Malcolm Barker

First published in 2000 by
Smith Settle Ltd
Ilkley Road
Otley
West Yorkshire
LS21 3JP

ISBN 1 85825 127 3

Set in Centaur.

Designed, printed and bound by
SMITH SETTLE
Ilkley Road, Otley, West Yorkshire LS21 3JP

Contents

Acknowledgements

I owe a great debt to both my grandfather, William Groves Barker MBE (1874-1950), and my father, Thomas Groves Barker (1903-1970), who between them edited the *Whitby Gazette* for forty-eight years from 1920 to 1968, and who built up a Henry Freeman archive which was eventually passed to me. Thanks, also, to Phil Pledger, the current *Gazette* editor, who delved into the bound files on my behalf, and to my old friend Mrs Patricia Frampton, who pointed the way to some invaluable illustrations, along with Mr Des Sythes, who looks after the Whitby Literary and Philosophical Society's splendid photographic collection.

For permission to reproduce the pictures on the cover and pages 2 and 12, I am indebted to Mr Michael J Shaw of the Sutcliffe Gallery in Flowergate, Whitby; and for those on pages 25, 36 and 37 to the joint honorary keepers of the Whitby Literary and Philosophical Society's Museum in Pannett Park, Whitby, Mr R L Pickles and Mr J G Pickles. Thanks, too, to Mr John Freeman for permission to reproduce his print of the 1881 lifeboat pull on page 32; and Mr F H Mason for his watercolour of the lifeboat launch on page 33.

I am also grateful to Kathleen Rainford, the former librarian for Yorkshire Post Newspapers Ltd in Leeds, the Royal National Lifeboat Institution, Patricia Sheldon of the Newcastle-upon-Tyne City Library, and the late Derek Naylor, feature writer for the *Yorkshire Evening Post*.

Research entailed many happy hours in the Whitby Literary and Philosophical Society's library, where help was always at hand from a great team including Mr Harold Brown BEM, Mrs Marian Durrans, Mrs Margaret Denham, Mrs Roma Hodgson, Mr Syd Barnett, Mrs Monica Ventress and Mrs J M Humble, whose gift of her late husband's papers is a prime source for anyone interested in Henry Freeman.

To my wife, Janet, without whom, nothing.

Portrait of a Lifeboat Hero

The Bulwark

One of the favourite subjects of the internationally-famous Whitby photographer Frank Meadow Sutcliffe was a well-built bearded fisherman with a determined upthrust to his chin, and eyes which usually appear to be raised to a distant horizon.

Sutcliffe posed him for portraits which remain bestsellers, and he figures in several of the more casual photographs taken at the harbourside and the fish market. In one group he appears third from left in a line of nine men passing the time of day against the harbour railings. It is to his figure that the eye is invariably drawn, a bulwark of a man with an oilskin cap on his head, and a leather waistcoat fastened only at the top button. His chest is enclosed in a knitted guernsey, and his legs in rumpled thigh-length sea boots. His is a striking figure, that of a man to whom others defer.

The widespread sale of prints of Sutcliffe's pictures from the Sutcliffe Gallery in Flowergate, Whitby, established by Bill Eglon Shaw after he had acquired the photographer's negatives in 1959, means that this fisherman has won extraordinary and posthumous fame. For many people, his is the image that instantly springs to mind if they try to visualise a Victorian seafarer.

The man on the photographs did not merely look the part. He was Henry Freeman, credited with saving more than 300 lives, Whitby lifeboat coxswain for more than a quarter of a century, the hero of epic rescues, a man honoured for his courage by the Royal National Lifeboat Institution, and admired by his fellow townsfolk.

Whitby Fishermen by the Harbour Rail, *a photograph by Frank Meadow Sutcliffe. Henry Freeman (third from the left) and John Batchelor (sixth from the left) are among some of the familiar faces which appear on other of Sutcliffe's photos of Whitby fisherfolk. (Sutcliffe Gallery.)*

Among those who have recognised the dramatic quality in his life was the playwright Peter Terson, who, in 1970, made him the principal character in a script based on a lifeboat disaster of 1861, of which Freeman was the sole survivor. In 1986, pupils at Whitby School (now the Whitby Community College) discovered that his grave was unmarked, and raised money for a headstone.

In 1991, Ray Shill, a British Rail stores controller, and Ian Minter, a schoolteacher, who both live in the Birmingham area, brought out his biography, *Storm Warrior* (Heartland Press, £16.50), an authoritative work

Henry Freeman's grave.

which resulted from years of painstaking research. Interest has not abated, and intensified with the re-enactment in 1999 of a famous rescue carried out under Freeman's leadership when, in wintry conditions in 1881, the Whitby lifeboat was hauled overland to Robin Hoods Bay to save the crew of a brig driven ashore during a tremendous storm. On the initiative of Mr Tony Vasey, a plaque has been placed in Cliff Street, Whitby, near the site of a cottage where Freeman spent part of his life.

Freeman was a big man in all senses of the word. At six foot three inches (1.9m) tall and weighing sixteen stones (100kg), he was an impressive sight as he strode the quay in thigh boots, with baited lines balanced on skeps, or wooden trays, slung over his broad shoulders. He is usually grim-visaged on photographs, so it is a pleasant surprise to find a comparatively rare shot in which he appears bare-headed, with a slightly frivolous quiff, and a mischievous twinkle in his eyes (see frontispiece). This reveals an aspect of his character which caused a *Whitby Gazette* obituarist to refer to his 'freehearted rollicking personality, gentle with children, for whom he always had a pat on the head'.

His image was of a kind sought after by manufacturers anxious to associate bold and fearless seamen with their goods. Weatherbeaten features resembling his were chosen to appear nationwide on tins of Skipper Sardines, a brand launched by Angus Watson (later Sir Angus) who set up a tinned goods business in Sunderland. Some thought it was indeed Freeman, but a copy of the Angus Watson house magazine in the Newcastle City Library archives identifies their 'Old Salt' as D W Anderson.

The power of Henry Freeman's personality was such that when he died aged sixty-nine, on the 13th December 1904, as a wild nor'-easter drove roaring seas across the harbour bar and rattled the pantiled roofs of the old town, some people simply could not believe that he had gone. There was reference to this in the *Whitby Gazette,* and the Rev E W Challenger, who preached at his funeral service at the Primitive Methodist church in Church Street, said that as the coffin was borne across the bridge covered by a Union Jack, he had instinctively looked towards the harbour railings expecting to see Freeman's sturdy frame.

An Off-comed 'Un

Henry Freeman's feat in capturing the respect of Whitby was all the more noteworthy because he was what was called 'a foreigner'. Fishing communities in the nineteenth century were close-knit groups of families. Whitby was no exception, with its Storrs, Harlands, Leadleys and Drydens. Their insularity was such that people from neighbouring villages like Robin Hoods Bay, Staithes and Runswick Bay were regarded as outsiders, an attitude which persisted into the twentieth century, as demonstrated by Leo Walmsley in his book *Three Fevers,* and is not unknown today. Freeman came from somewhere even more distant than these villages. He was born at Bridlington in April 1835, and not into a fishing family either. His

The West Pier and Lighthouse at Whitby, *a lithograph most probably the work of F Nicholson. It was from the slipway on the left, between the pier and the battery, that the lifeboat was launcheed.* (Whitby Prints)

parents married at Eastrington, a farming village in the East Riding of Yorkshire, and although they moved to Bridlington, they had no business with the sea. Henry's father, William, was a brickmaker, a trade in which Henry himself served an apprenticeship, and when he moved to Whitby at the age of twenty, that was the occupation he intended to follow.

But business was slack, and after making four trips on coasters to the Thames, he decided to join the 700 or more Whitby men who earned a precarious living by fishing inshore waters from a fleet of small boats, the traditional East coast cobles. These facts emerge from the *Whitby Gazette* obituary, but those early years remain tantalisingly obscure.

However, it is not surprising that seagoing appealed to the well-built young tradesman. Whitby was a thriving port in the mid-nineteenth century. An Admiralty surveyor's report for 1844 conjures a vision of great activity. No fewer than fourteen building slips lined the banks of the Esk, and echoed to the ring of adze on seasoned timber as new ships took shape, and were readied for launching. In addition there were seven repairing docks, from which the jib-booms of vessels reached out across the harbourside streets.

Fifty thousand tons of shipping belonged to the port. The harbour was thronged, with 2,000 arrivals and sailings every year. It also served as a refuge. As many as seventy-five ships in search of shelter entered on a single tide. When the threat of severe weather lifted, they crowded between the piers on their way out to the sea-lanes, sometimes 100 to a tide. It was also a time of great expansion in the inshore fishing industry. At the beginning of the century, Whitby had fewer than a score of cobles which were licensed, presumably for salmon fishing. By the 1860s, there were more than 120.

All this was surely enough to spark the imagination of a lively lad like young Freeman. His emergence from the shadows into lifeboat history came on Saturday the 9th February 1861. Dawn that day found him on the beach walking towards Sandsend in company with six fishermen, John Storr, John Dixon, Robert Leadley, William Tyreman, George Martin and William Dryden. Freeman then was twenty-five years of age, and presumably already a coble fisherman.

A full gale was blowing from the north-east that morning, and at about eight o'clock, an hour before low water, the seven men walking the shore saw that a brig, later identified as the *John and Ann* of Sunderland, had been driven ashore. Realising that the crew would be in danger when the tide turned, they took a Sandsend coble and brought the sailors off the stricken vessel. They would inevitably have taken their lead from John Storr, steersman of the Whitby lifeboat, and possessor of a formidable reputation not only for courage, but also for skill as a boat-handler. The *John and Ann* rescue may have been Freeman's first experience of life-saving. Unlike his six colleagues, he was not a lifeboatman.

The Great Storm

The rescue of the men brought ashore from the *John and Ann* raised the curtain on a day of intense drama, consummate gallantry and ultimate tragedy.

From the start the portents were ominous. In those days there was an intensive coasting trade, with a vast fleet of sailing ships carrying coal from the Tyne to the Thames. These colliers, often old, leaky and inadequately crewed, were frighteningly vulnerable if caught by a gale against a lee shore. Appalled by the losses they sustained, Admiral Robert Fitzroy, a great humanitarian, meteorologist and hydrographer, was in the process of setting up a system of weather forecasting in his capacity as chief of the meteorological department at the Board of Trade.

On the 6th February he caused a warning to be telegraphed to principal ports: 'Caution — gale threatening from the south-west and then northward.' Alas, in the words of the *Annual Register* for 1861, master mariners in the Tyne 'totally disregarded the intimation'. On Friday the 8th February at least 100 of them sailed from there, and began a voyage in company with as many again from neighbouring ports. As the threatened storm intensified, disaster befell this fleet of small, heavily-laden sailing ships. There were heavy losses down the East Coast, as many were driven ashore and pounded to matchwood. Even in a country accustomed to losses at sea, the catastrophe made its mark, contributing vastly to the 1,498 wrecks recorded round the coasts of the British Isles in 1861.

It was the outriders of this ill-fated armada, vessels that had set sail on Thursday the 7th February, that came to grief off Whitby.

The men involved in the *John and Ann* rescue must have realised that further lifesaving endeavours would be required of them. In the words of the *Whitby Gazette*: 'The large fleet of sailing vessels known to be on the coast caused grave fears that serious calamities might occur.' With the exception of William Dryden, who had to attend to his coble, they went to the Whitby lifeboat house after walking back along the shore from Sandsend. They found the lifeboat being made ready for service. It was a new vessel, built in the town by Francis Falkingbridge, and paid for by subscription.

Then, at about ten o'clock, the signal gun boomed amid the uproar of the storm. The schooner *Gamma,* laden with coals for London, was on the beach some 400 yards (365m) from West Pier, and in imminent danger of breaking up. Four heavy horses hauled the lifeboat on its carriage along Pier Road and down the slipway between the pier and Battery Parade. She was launched from the beach, as was usual in those days, and John Storr took charge as steersman. There was a place for Henry Freeman in the twelve-man crew despite his lack of lifeboat experience. Perhaps John Storr had been impressed by the brawny youngster's part in the earlier rescue.

He certainly did not get in for want of volunteers. Throughout that terrible day there seems to have been keen competition to get in the boat,

A rowing lifeboat of the mid-nineteenth century. (RNLI.)

and twice she put to sea with thirteen men aboard against a complement of twelve, an oddity indeed in a fishing community ridden by superstition.

With four men safely ashore from the *Gamma*, the next call was to a Prussian barque, the *Clara*, Sunderland-built and on passage from Newcastle to Madeira. She was a larger vessel with deeper draught, and consequently grounded a good distance from the shore. Her crew of eleven took to the rigging as tumultuous seas swept clean over her. The lifeboatmen faced a test of strength as well as courage. Soaked to the skin, and hauling at oars with hands numbed by cold, they were frequently driven back, and it was with immense difficulty that John Storr eventually got alongside. Eleven men were plucked to safety, and not before time, because the *Clara* soon broke up and simply disappeared.

The rescue completed, the lifeboat was replaced on her carriage to await further calls, which seemed inevitable. During this respite, John Storr had a conversation with the harbourmaster, William Tose, about the new boat's performance. He complained that she was too narrow, and as a result the men lacked space to exert full leverage on the oars. Tose later recalled him saying: 'If we had to pull off with a heavy sea, it would tire any man to get her off.'

In the early afternoon, with the spring tide still flowing and no abatement in the severity of the weather, two more vessels were flung ashore, the brig *Utility* and the schooner *Roe*. The lifeboat took off their crews in a single operation, and returned safely. But with high water due at 3.57pm, and great waves surging in, the lifeboat could not be left on the beach. Once again she was manhandled on to her carriage and hauled up the slipway.

It seemed likely that another rescue mission would be impossible until after the tide had turned, for high water made launching down the slipway difficult, and landing virtually impossible, but, at two o'clock, two schooners were sighted through the welter of flying spume and broken water. They were being driven ashore under bare poles. One of them, the *Flora* of London, by luck or a remarkable feat of seamanship, passed to safety

The instant of disaster, as the lifeboat is caught in 'a knot of the sea'— a contemporary representation which appeared in the Illustrated London News.

through the harbour entrance. But to the dismay of a vast crowd of onlookers, her companion in distress, the *Merchant* of Maldon, Essex, came ashore no more than forty yards (36m) from the pier, and a similar distance seaward of the battery. Her master, George Young, later recalled that, on striking, her crew had taken to the rigging, but even there the sea was 'making clean breaches over them'. The sea was full of wreckage, with ships' timbers tossing about like matchsticks, and close inshore the remains of the *Roe* were being beaten to bits. It was a daunting prospect even for

John Storr, whose initial reaction was that a launch would serve no useful purpose, But the crew's blood was up, and Storr formulated a plan which, though fraught with peril, offered sufficient chance of success to make the risk worthwhile. He got the boat into the water and, with his gallant men, once again braved the terrific storm.

The Sole Survivor

Somehow John Storr steered to the *Merchant,* only for the lifeboat to be driven back when cross seas formed where waves surged round the stricken vessel. This happened on at least two occasions, but the lifeboatmen continued to bend resolutely to their oars. But the sea was turbulent beyond ordinary experience. Vast waves driving shoreward met others rebounding either off wrecks or the masonry of battery and pier. As the waves dashed about in furious confusion, the inshore waters were a cauldron. Even so, John Storr and his twelve crewmen came tantalisingly close to effecting a rescue. George Young, the *Merchant*'s master, later said that the lifeboat had been near enough for one of the crew to strike the stern of the schooner with a boathook, presumably in the hope of grappling alongside. Also, the *Merchant*'s mate was ready to try and get a rope across to the lifeboat, but a fleeting opportunity passed when the lifeboat was whisked past her stern.

Suddenly there was a congress of waves, a coming together of surges travelling in opposite directions. Water was flung up in what sailormen call 'a knot of the sea'. The lifeboat, caught at the crux of this collision, hurtled skywards, clearing the water according to some eye-witness accounts. She was then caught broad-side on, and turned right over. Two men, William Tyreman and Isaac Dobson, were trapped underneath. The other eleven were flung into the sea. There, in full view of an agonised multitude, among them their wives, children and mothers, the heroes struggled for their lives, battling with the fury of the breakers until one by one their struggles ended. Men threw lifebelts, and spars from the capstans on the pier, and the rocket fired lines. One brave man jumped from the pier with a rope round him to try to save any within reach, but he had to be hauled

High Seas on Whitby's West Pier *by Frank Meadow Sutcliffe. The photograph was taken before the addition of the extensions to the piers, built around 1912. At that time the full force of the sea was taken by the much older stone piers. It was from the pier and the slipway to the left that many brave attempts were made to rescue the drowning lifeboatmen in the February 1861 disaster. (Sutlcliffe Gallery.)*

up again at once, or he would have been dashed to pieces against the stonework.

Later, at the battery, another man with a rope round him waded into the seething waters to try to help one of the crew seen floating near the beach. Both were dashed with great force against the stones of the slipway, and, brave though this action was, it only served to bring in the dead body of Matthew Leadley. In the words of a correspondent of the *Yorkshire Gazette:* 'The sights, the shrieks, the moans, the anxiety of mind, will not readily be forgotten: to see the poor men floating about, and no assistance could be rendered to them.'

John Storr, brave and resourceful to the last, somehow managed to scramble face-down on to the upturned boat. The sea clawed at him. Eventually, he was spun over on his back and, after hanging on for a few moments, he too was swept to his death. When his body was recovered, it was discovered that he had a broken arm, and the *Leeds Intelligencer* aired the theory that he had sought to strengthen his grasp on the boat by thrusting his arm into a hole in the hull.

The lifeboat, which from the first had been keel upwards, slowly drifted in. Men with hatchets rushed into the sea and smashed their way into the hull, hoping to save the two men trapped underneath. Both, however, were dead on landing.

At the moment of capsize, Henry Freeman was also trapped, pinned by the gunwale across his chest. Late in his life he recalled:

> My body was under the boat and I was looking upwards through the water. A sea struck the boat and released me and I floated free.
>
> I was wearing a new type of cork belt, which had been sent down for trial. There was a ship wrecked up against the pier and every now and then this ship was being banged by the waves against the pier. I was driven along towards this wreck, and I was afraid every second that I was going to be crushed between the ship and the pier, but a big sea came and a carried me safe between the ship and the pier side, and then I was washed towards the slipway.
>
> A wave carried me right to the top, and several men tried to get hold of me, but a strong backwash took me out to sea again. Another sea then took me right up the slipway again, but I was washed down again. Then, a third time I was carried up the slipway, and this time some men got hold of me and I was then half carried up the pier home.
>
> I was proper done up.

None of the other twelve men survived. Whitby's grief at this bereavement was communicated to the outside world by the town's rector, the Rev

William Keane, who sat down later that evening and wrote a heartfelt letter to *The Times*:

> Will you allow your newspaper to add another tale of anguish to the many which have recently called forth the sympathy of the public? We have had a fearful storm today at Whitby. Half-a-mile of our strand is already strewed with seven wrecks. Our new lifeboat, was but launched a few months ago, and was manned with the old crew of the finest picked seamen in Whitby. Five times during the day had they braved the furious sea and five times returned with crews from vessels in distress. A sixth ship was driven in behind the pier. The men, all exhausted though they were, again pulled out, but before they had gone fifty yards a wave capsized the boat. Then was beheld by several thousand persons — within almost a stone's throw, but unable to assist — the fearful agonies of those powerful men buffeting with the fury of the breakers, till one by one twelve out of thirteen sank, and only one is saved.
>
> I have to add that eleven out of these twelve were married and have left families, and I am sorry to say that I myself know that owing to the severe winter to fishermen nearly all are left destitute. Whitby will do its duty to its bravest hands, but I feel assured that an old lifeboat's crew who have saved hundreds of our fellow creatures from such a fate as this, and at last perished in the noble discharge of duty to the public, will have the wants of their bereaved families cared for by the readers of *The Times* — Saturday night, the 9th February 1861.

Despite the loss of its lifeboat crew, Whitby continued to help mariners driven ashore by that frightful storm. The five-man crew of the *Merchant* was brought to safety after a mortar had been used to throw a line across the vessel. With the tide ebbing, a brig *Urania* came ashore as daylight faded. A rocket line was got across her, but the crew decided to stay aboard until she was high and dry.

After nightfall, a small brig, the 132-ton *Tribune,* grounded not far from the West Pier. Her master, Nicholas Browse of Brixham, later gave a vivid account of the peril of being at sea during the storm:

> Five pm saw Whitby light, very hazy, sea running fearfully high, wind ENE blowing a hurricane. Finding the ship would not weather Whitby Rock, ran for the harbour, but recollecting there was not sufficient water, put vessel on the north side of pier. The crew took to the rigging.

Initially, attempts were made to get a line across the *Tribune,* but these failed. The cries of the crew could be heard on the shore, and a desperate situation was met with a desperate remedy. A volunteer crew, including six master mariners and two jet ornament-makers, took the old East Side lifeboat into the breakers, and saved all but one man, who was thought to have

The aftermath of the 'Great Storm' on Sunday the 10th February 1861. (Richard Weatherill's Ancient Port of Whitby and its Shipping.*)*

drowned after trying to jump into the lifeboat. The old boat was used again next morning when the brig *Memnon* was pitched on the beach towards Sandsend, and her complement was brought ashore safely. That was the last spasm of a storm which littered the East Coast with wrecks, seventy of them near Hartlepool, where ten ships were lost with all hands.

Aftermath

In John Storr, Whitby had lost a man described as the best lifeboatman the town ever had. Of him it was said: 'If John Storr would take charge, the men did not consider any risk too great for his steady watchful eye and powerful arm.' He was fifty-three years of age, a patriarch of the fishing community. His brother, Will, who acted as assistant steersman for the *Merchant* launch, perished with him, together with John Dixon, Robert Leadley, Robert Harland, William Walker, Isaac Dobson, John Philpot, Will Tyreman, Matt Leadley, George Martin and Christopher Collins.

Together they had years of experience of the coast and the hazards of rescue work, and to some it may have seemed strange that the sole survivor of the crew was a man taking his oar in the lifeboat for the first time that day, an off-comed 'un who had not even been born a fisherman. That is probably why, at the time and ever since, Henry Freeman's survival has been attributed not to his courage, strength, determination and, yes, good fortune, but to the type of lifejacket he was wearing.

The older belts tended to chafe the men under their arms as they plied their oars, and for that reason they wore them low down, 'round their waists', according to the *Leeds Intelligencer.* Only one crewman, Robert Leadley, was not wearing a belt of any kind. Freeman's new belt, which possibly fell to him as the newest recruit, had been sent as a sample. At the subsequent inquest, he told the coroner, John Buchanan, that he had found it in the boat. Years later he posed for a photograph in the belt which, according to the caption, was the one he had used. Braced around his chest are seven segments of cork, flanked at either side by shorter segments under the arms. A belt, secured round the waist, holds the cork segments in place from below, and supports further segments round the lower part of the trunk.

Freeman wore the belt for all four launches, and it was still in position when a human chain plucked him from the sea on the slipway. Exhausted, bruised, and half-drowned, he was taken home to Bolton's Buildings in Cliff Street, where he was lodging with Mrs Margaret Snowden.

The lifebelt designed by Capt Ward RN, inspector of lifeboats for the RNLI, which was worn by Henry Freeman and undoubtedly helped save his life. (RNLI)

By the Monday afternoon, he had recovered sufficiently to give evidence at the inquest. He told the coroner that on the day of the storm he had had nothing to eat since breakfast, and did not think that the other men had either. They had, however, gone for a glass of grog after each of the first three launches.

These tots of rum, more or less diluted with water, taken on a cruel February day by men subjecting themselves to hard physical labour, hardly seem the subject for comment. Even taken on empty stomachs, their effect would surely be offset by the sheer effort of pulling the lifeboat. There was nothing in the coroner's summing up or the jury's verdict to indicate that drink was worth considering as a contributory factor in the tragedy. The jurymen returned verdicts of 'accidentally drowned', and added a rider making a strong recommendation 'that in future efficient life-belts, similar to the one used by Henry Freeman, be adopted'.

Freeman's evidence assumed greater importance two weeks later when a temperance lecturer called Thomas Whittaker had a letter printed in the *Scarborough Mercury* attributing the lifeboat disaster to drunkenness. He wrote that the men had 'from mistaken kindness, been supplied, in some cases freely so, with spirits, by which more than one of them had left that self-control and sobriety essential to safety in such a storm'. In making this statement, Whittaker must have been relying on gossip. He chose to ignore evidence given at the inquest by the harbourmaster, William Tose, that although some of the men 'would have a little liquor in them', they were all competent to put to sea. In this he was supported by Captain Butler RN who, unlike Whittaker, was on the scene and saw nothing remarkable about the behaviour of the crew.

The allegations against the lifeboatmen were deeply resented, and, in the case of John Storr, manifestly absurd, for he was known not to take a drink. Nor was the outrage confined to Whitby. In Scarborough, 5,000 gathered to demonstrate against Whittaker, relieving their feelings by hanging an effigy labelled WHITE-E-CUR from a gibbet. This contrivance was paraded round the town by sailors, and belaboured by two men swinging cats-o'-nine-tails. On the beach, opposite the lifeboat house, they set it on fire, and the crowd cheered as it burned.

A far more judicial rebuttal of Whittaker's allegations came from A F Humble in his *The Rowing Lifeboats of Whitby* (Hornes, 1974). He pointed out that the Royal National Lifeboat Institution, which was not responsible for life-saving in Whitby at that time, was anxious to distance itself from the disaster, thus preserving the morale of its own crews. In doing so, it could have achieved its purpose by attributing the tragedy to some failure on the part of the Whitby men, poor boatmanship, or insobriety.

Instead the RNLI contented itself with pointing out that the only survivor, Henry Freeman, 'was the only one who had an efficient life-belt', of a type designed by Capt Ward RN, their inspector of lifeboats, which was always worn on service by RNLI crews. Also, the Falkingbridge boat had not been built to RNLI specifications, and had not been under RNLI management.

So far as the Whitby men were concerned, in March of 1861 the institution took a far more positive step, paying tribute to the dead heroes by saluting the lone survivor.

A Novice Hero

The RNLI announced that Henry Freeman, a comparative newcomer to the fishing community, and a novice lifeboatman, was to get its silver medal. A seaman called Thomas Robinson was similarly honoured for the gallantry he had shown in attempting to save the lives of the two men who had been trapped under the lifeboat in the capsize, in the process of which he had suffered a severe hand injury.

When Captain Ward, the RNLI's inspector of boats, made the presentation on the 12th April 1861, it must have seemed to many still in mourning that, in giving Freeman such resounding recognition, the institution was pinning its medal on the only chest still available to represent the whole crew. All that could be done by way of honouring the other men was by the provision of a memorial. This took the form of a curious pagoda-like structure, supposedly bought secondhand by the rector of Whitby, which now stands in the parish church of St Mary on the abbey cliff.

Henry Freeman was undoubtedly fortunate to receive such early recognition. But he had demonstrated possession of a quality which was as much esteemed within the fishing community as courage, strength and determination. Henry Freeman was lucky. He was a man to follow.

It was a reputation which lasted a lifetime. His obituary described him as 'singularly fortunate in many respects'. It was not that he earned large sums of money ('unfortunately for him that was not the case'), but when the fleet of cobles put to sea and he led the way, it was 'tolerably certain that fish would be found nearest his boat'.

Freeman emerged as Whitby's least experienced and most decorated lifeboatman, and began an association with lifesaving — which was to continue until his retirement — at the time when the RNLI set up its first branch in the town. The loss of the crew had persuaded Whitby that the time had come to abandon its independence in the supervision of arrangements for lifesaving at sea.

Edward Chapman, a member of a prominent shipping family, became the first to hold the important post of RNLI secretary in Whitby. In the early years, he and his colleagues faced the aggravation of competition from a private lifeboat which was called the *Fishermen's Friend*. Among its shareholders were experienced lifeboatmen, who were therefore not available to join the port's RNLI crews. John Pickering was the local committee's first coxswain-superintendent. During April 1861, the month when the newly-formed committee of the Whitby branch of the RNLI held its first meeting, Pickering collected a new thirty-two feet (8m) self-righting boat, the *Lucy*, from the railway station and took her on sea trials.

For the rest of the 1860s, Henry Freeman's name appears from time to time in lifeboat records, and he continued to work as a fisherman. In 1870 Harry Freeman, as the *Whitby Gazette* called him, brought in Whitby's first herring catch of the season on the 15th June, 1,000 fish which made 1s 6d ($7^1/_2$p) a hundred. That same year he acquired his own coble, and called it *William and Margaret* after his father and mother. Two years later this vessel capsized and sank during a coble race, with the loss of one man in the three-strong crew. Henry Freeman was not aboard, and publicly denied that the race was any of his doing.

Coxswain Freeman

Freeman's first command was the Upgang lifeboat, called *William Watson*, which was based on the foreshore between Whitby and Sandsend. The cliffs there are boulder clay, which is eroded relentlessly by the sea, and the boat was housed in a brick-built shed at the head of a slipway at the recommendation of the local RNLI committee, who believed it would be capable of being launched even when a north-easterly gale rendered a launch at Whitby impossible.

The new coxswain's appointment in 1875 did not receive universal acclaim. He was at odds with Samuel Lacy, John Pickering's successor as

Launching the Life Boat, *an engraving by Thomas Prior after a watercolour by Edwin Duncan. It shows the lifeboat going out at night from Upgang to a ship lying between Upgang and Whitby, and in the background the Mulgrave Inn at Upgang (now gone into the sea), with Whitby Abbey and the Royal Crescent.* (Whitby Prints.)

Whitby coxswain, who seems to have persistently ignored Freeman when choosing his crew, and the bad feeling between the men soon surfaced in a way which must have angered and embarrassed the local members of the RNLI.

Lacy had launched the lifeboat *Robert Whitworth* after a dismasted ship had been sighted adrift in heavy seas. When the lifeboat reached her after a long and difficult pull, she proved to be a derelict, with no souls on board. The exhausted lifeboatmen beached the *Robert Whitworth* at Runswick Bay. When they were bringing her home two days later, they encountered a barque called the *Svadsfare* flying distress signals.

This ship in distress had been sighted from Whitby, and Henry Freeman, with a pilot and other fishermen, launched a coble to go to her aid. They arrived too late, for when they reached the vessel, Samuel Lacy and the lifeboat crew were already alongside, and, after the idea of beaching the

Svadsfare had been abandoned, had arranged to escort her to harbour. The *Robert Whitworth* and her charge headed for Hartlepool, leaving the dispirited coble crew to pull back to Whitby through heavy seas, their hopes of salvage money dashed.

It was all too much. The coblemen wrote a letter to the Royal National Lifeboat Institution in London, complaining that, by taking possession of the *Svadsfare*, Samuel Lacy had used the RNLI's *Robert Whitworth* in opposition to private enterprise which, they asserted, was 'contrary to the Institution's regulations, and is in effect taking the bread from our families'. For good measure, they accused Lacy of leaving them in extreme peril to get back to Whitby as well as they could.

To ensure that their disgruntlement was aired locally, they sent a copy of this letter for publication to the *Whitby Times*. The five signatories were led by John Duncan, a pilot, and the third in the list was Henry Freeman, described as 'Fisherman and coxswain of the Upgang lifeboat', although he was later to deny even having seen the letter. If this assertion arouses incredulity, it must be remembered that, like many of his contemporaries, Freeman was illiterate. To the end of his life, he was making his mark with a cross. What he probably meant was that he had not read the letter, the simple truth, because he could not. *The Times* printed a rebuttal the following week from George Smales, the Whitby branch RNLI secretary, revealing the extent of the rift between the town's lifesavers.

Samuel Lacy had the immediate support of the local RNLI committee and ultimately of the RNLI's inspector of boats, who carried out an enquiry. He cautioned Freeman, but allowed him to continue as coxswain of the Upgang boat, a lenient decision surely, for the notorious letter had threatened to use the private lifeboat, the *Fishermen's Friend*, against the RNLI boats whenever the opportunity arose.

Freeman never launched the Upgang boat on service. Indeed, according to Mr Humble's *The Rowing Lifeboats of Whitby*, it only answered two serious calls in the entire history of the station, which closed when Whitby acquired its first motor lifeboat after the First World War. However, Freeman

The Whitby No 2 lifeboat, the Harriott Forteath. *There were two consecutive lifeboats stationed at Whitby which were both named after their donor Mrs Forteath of Nottingham.* *(RNLI)*

soon had the opportunity to demonstrate his mettle by taking the Whitby No 1 lifeboat, *Robert Whitworth,* out. The occasion arose in May 1876, because Samuel Lacy, his old adversary, was at sea fishing. Indeed, the rescuer needed rescuing, for his coble had been upset in high seas, and the Whitby second coxswain, Thomas Hartley, had taken the No 2 lifeboat, *Harriott Forteath,* to save Lacy and his companions. Meanwhile, another coble was seen to be in difficulty, giving Freeman the chance to launch the *Robert Whitworth* and effect a rescue.

On the 10th January 1877 came another lifeboat tragedy. In the early hours, Samuel Lacy took the *Harriott Forteath* to the rescue of the crew of a small ketch, the *Agenoria,* which had gone ashore a quarter of a mile from the West Pier and was being beaten to pieces on the sand. Lacy launched in enormous seas in pitch darkness. Meanwhile the harbourmaster, Robert Gibson, and coastguards had manhandled rocket apparatus down the cliff near the wreck and, having got a line across her, they managed to get the three-man crew to safety. By the light of a rocket, they had a glimpse of *Harriott Forteath* making her way towards what remained of *Agenoria.*

The next thing the men on shore knew of the lifeboat must have shocked them to the core. A wave swept in, depositing a lifeboatman at their feet. As they dragged him clear and he struggled to his feet, they recognised him as John Storr, whose father died in the 1861 disaster. The *Harriott Forteath,* with a drogue, or sea anchor, out, had been heading shorewards in her search for the wreck when a huge wave broke right underneath her, filling her to the gunwales and overwhelming her. All the crew were thrown overboard with the exception of one man, and he was still aboard when the *Harriott Forteath* righted herself. Others scrambled back over the gunwales, but three were missing, and cries for help could still be heard in the darkness.

They all drowned: brave Samuel Lacy, the coxswain, aged forty-nine, Thomas Gatenby, father of six and the hero of many rescues, and John Thompson, aged twenty-eight.

It was Gatenby's death which threw a poignant light on the fears of the families of Whitby lifeboatmen of that era. When Mrs Gatenby was told her husband was drowned, her thoughts turned immediately to ways and means of providing for the children she had, and the seventh she was expecting. She told her friend her best course would be to 'keep a mangle', if only she could raise the means of purchasing one. Hearing of this, a Whitby woman responded instantly — by promising Mrs Gatenby the best mangle in town.

The death of Samuel Lacy gave Henry Freeman his chance. Amid some acrimony, the town's RNLI branch committee appointed him Whitby coxswain by a majority vote.

The Heroic Years

Hardly surprisingly in light of the animosity revealed by the exchange of letters in the *Whitby Times,* one of Henry Freeman's most vehement opponents on the lifeboat committee was the secretary, George Smales, who resigned in protest at the appointment. This the committee refused to accept, and two days later produced a formula designed to keep both men in office Their resolution was: 'that Mr Smales be requested to continue to act as secretary, the committee undertaking to relieve him of all responsibility arising from the appointment of Henry Freeman'.

The Return of the Lifeboat *by Edward Duncan, engraved by Arthur Willmore and published in 1876. (Whitby Literary & Philosophical Society.)*

There was also a problem with George Hartley, the second coxswain, who had been a friend and colleague of Samuel Lacy, and was an experienced lifeboatman with an unblemished reputation who might reasonably have looked to the committee for promotion. He resolutely refused to serve under Freeman.

Obviously, opponents would call the new coxswain's judgement into question and the *Svadsfare* affair rankled with some, who thought he had shown disloyalty, but none could question Freeman's courage, and he soon demonstrated that he had the personality required to lead a successful crew of lifesavers, who quickly became noted for their skill and gallantry.

Within three weeks of Freeman's appointment, they had saved fifteen lives. In the first three years, this total increased to sixty. In October 1880,

A turn-of-the-century pulling and sailing lifeboat. A vessel of this type, the Robert and Ellen Robson, *is preserved at the Whitby Lifeboat Museum on West Pier. (RNLI.)*

during a storm so ferocious that houses in Whitby were blown over, Freeman led his men in a series of four rescues which earned him a second RNLI bravery award, a silver clasp to add to the silver medal he had received in 1861.

The account of these events published in the RNLI's summary of services gives a telling insight into the hazards which faced the rescuers:

> On October 28, about noon, a vessel was observed to be fast drifting on to Whitby Rocks. She, however, succeeded in clearing the rocks, and was driven with tremendous force on the beach. The wind was then blowing a hurricane from the ENE, and the sea was extremely high. The lifeboat *Robert Whitworth* put off to her assistance, and with great difficulty and danger succeeded in rescuing her crew, consisting

of four men. She proved to be the schooner *Reaper*, of Douglas, bound from Ostend to Sunderland, in ballast.

At 1.20 pm, a large fishing yawl, the *Good Intent*, of Staithes, was observed running for Whitby sands, and as it was evident she was in great distress, the lifeboat again put off through a fearful sea, and, with great danger and difficulty, saved the crew, consisting of eight men.

At 3.15 pm the schooner, *Elizabeth Austin*, of Rye, bound thence for Sunderland in ballast, was seen to be drifting rapidly towards the beach. The lifeboat was immediately launched, and, upon the vessel stranding, her crew of five men were with difficulty taken into the lifeboat, and brought safely ashore.

At 4.30 pm, the schooner *John Snell*, of Great Yarmouth, bound thence to Newcastle with a cargo of wheat, was also seen to be making for the beach. It was feared she would not succeed in reaching the shore, as the tremendous seas continually swept over her, completely hiding her from view at times. She fortunately, however, kept her steerage-way and eventually struck the beach. The lifeboat, after being pulled for some distance through a seething mass of broken water, ultimately reached the vessel, and succeeded in landing her crew, consisting of five men.

With rescues like this being widely reported, Freeman emerged as a Victorian hero. His fame took many forms. A magazine, the *Cottager and the Artisan*, which described itself in surprisingly modern terms as 'The People's Own Paper', used his picture on the cover, and again inside, when it featured 'Heroes of the Lifeboat'. A Mrs Frederick Campbell was moved to have a photographic copy made of G F Watts' painting *Love and Death*, which she sent to Freemen with a message solicited from the artist himself, who avowed that heroic lifeboatmen were 'maintaining the character of the nation at its noblest.' Freeman might have been happier with a plug of black twist, for he enjoyed puffing at a clay pipe, or, better still, a fine cigar, which was his special treat.

Overland to Bay

Henry Freeman's national fame was confirmed in 1881 with the rescue of the crew of the *Visitor* at Robin Hoods Bay, which entailed taking the lifeboat six miles (9.5km) overland.

The year began badly for the Whitby lifeboat crew. On Sunday the 15th January, a brig called the *Lumley* of South Shields came ashore on Upgang Rock. Her distress signal was seen by a coastguard, and although both the Upgang and Whitby lifeboats were launched amid great peril, no rescue was effected, and the ten seaman on the *Lumley* were drowned.

There was deep sorrow in the town, and Freeman's qualities of leadership were required to raise the morale of his crew, which was an urgent matter, for the January gales persisted, and more calls on their services seemed inevitable. The *Lumley* gale was accompanied by heavy snow, which became frozen and lay two to three feet (0.6-0.9m) deep, making roads very difficult. Two days later, another south-easterly gale imperilled vessels in the coasting trade. By nightfall on Tuesday the 17th January, a gale was raging fiercely, with blinding showers of snow and hail. A sharp look-out was kept, but none of the vessels sighted off Whitby showed signs of distress.

But a call did come, and from an unexpected quarter. On the morning of Wednesday the 18th January, a telegram was received from Robin Hoods Bay, asking for assistance to be sent to the crew of a brig who had taken to their small boat and were out in the bay, exposed to the elements, and the fury of the sea. The vessel concerned was the *Visitor* of 203 tons, built at Sunderland in 1823, registered at Whitby and owned at Robin Hoods Bay by Trueman Robinson. This ancient collier had humbly plied the coal trade for more than half a century in total obscurity under a succession of owners, and even when her end secured her a kind of immortality, she still from time to time suffered — and still suffers — the indignity of having her name spelt wrongly as Visiter. Her last voyage is chronicled in succinct terms in Richard Weatherill's *The Ancient Port of Whitby and its Shipping* (Hornes, 1908):

'Visitor', owner Trueman Robinson, R H. Bay, Capt., Will Todd Anderson, and five hands, Shields for London, Jan 16th, 1881, with coals, 18th, close to Flambro' Head, when at 4 p.m, the wind changed and began to blow a gale from S.E. to E. with snow. During the night, blowing a gale, all the sails were blown away except the main trysail and the main staysail, and the ship drove North.

About 2 am. on the 19th sounded and found 20 fathoms. To prevent the ship driving ashore, brought up with both anchors down about 4 miles off R.H. Bay town, and on sounding the pumps found two feet of water in the vessel. The sea broke quite over the ship, the wind a hurricane from the East. About 8 am. found five feet of water in the hold, and to save life got out the long-boat, and all hands got into her, and hung by a kedge and two warps near the vessel.

Soon afterwards the vessel foundered. The crew continued in the boat until about 3 p.m., when the lifeboat, which had been brought from Whitby by land to R.H. Bay and here launched, came out and succeeded in rescuing the crew, who were so exhausted by exposure to the cold, that they had to be carried from the lifeboat to the shore at R.H. Bay. Ship a total loss.

Behind this straightforward and seamanlike account lies an extraordinary story. The fishermen at Robin Hoods Bay were unable to help as their lifeboat was old and unseaworthy, and to put to sea in her in the conditions which prevailed at the time would have meant swift and certain death. Although they were in their long-boat, and had some shelter in the lee of the wreck, the brig's crew could not possibly reach the shore through the breakers even if they had known how to navigate across the rocky scaur to the slipway, where there was a narrow seaway with which only Bay fishermen were familiar.

But the Bay men could not leave the *Visitor*'s crew to its fate. They agreed there was a chance — a slender one, but a chance. They would send a telegram to ask the Whitby lifeboatmen if there was anything they could do to help. The message sent by the Rev Jermyn Cooper, vicar of Fylingdales, was: 'Vessel sunk, crew in open boat riding by the wreck, send Whitby lifeboat if practicable.'

The Whitby crew was called together by Captain Gibson, harbourmaster and lifeboat secretary. What could be done? It might have been possible to go by sea, but by then a wind veering to the north-east whipped up enormous waves, and even if the lifeboat could have been towed part of the way, the sea passage offered scant hope of getting to Bay in time to save the *Visitor*'s men. Then an idea was thrown out: 'We'll take her by land'. Whether Freeman initiated this audacious scheme is not known, but he was certainly instrumental in its implementation.

To drag a heavy and unwieldy lifeboat over six miles (9.5km) of hilly road, feet deep in frozen snow through which a way would have to be cut with spades and axes, and all in the teeth of a gale and snow flurries — well, it may have seemed impossible.

But the spirit of Freeman and his crew was roused. They could not — would not — allow those poor fellows to perish without making an effort. The decision made, the enthusiasm of the townsfolk backed the resolve. Excitement spread as the lifeboat was mounted on her carriage, and hauled up Pier Road and across the bridge into Church Street.

The atmosphere of that day was caught many years later in an eyewitness account published in Dora M Walker's *Freemen of the Sea* (Brown and Sons, 1951). It was supplied by the son of an ironmonger with a shop in Church Street. That morning, he recalled, the snow lay so thick that his father had to carry him down to the shop. He was playing with a hammer and some chips of wood when some men burst into the shop: 'Their shoulders were white with snow and it blew in after them in a cloud as the door slammed. "Shovels!", they shouted, "Shovels and spades, all you've got. There's a ship ashore at Bay, and we're going to take the lifeboat overland".' The shop's entire stock was cleared and 'in a minute all the men were out in the roadway, sending the snow flying right and left, like terriers at a rabbit'.

The boy then saw the lifeboat, the *Robert Whitworth*, dragged along Church Street on its carriage, with Freeman in charge supported by the second coxswain, John Storr. By the time the cavalcade began the haul up Helredale, upwards of 100 men had turned out to help, and all their strength and determination were needed as the boat made the long ascent out of Whitby. Fair progress was achieved, and the pace improved when a couple of horses were brought out and harnessed to the carriage. Farmers, gripped by an infectious desire to help, turned out with more offers of horse-power, which were gladly accepted. When accounts were submitted to the RNLI, hire was paid for fourteen horses at 15s (75p) each.

The news that Freeman and his men were on their way had been telegraphed to Robin Hoods Bay, and men from the village tackled the frozen drifts. Among them was Matthew Wellburn, a local farmer, who was invited by Freeman and Captain Gibson to take charge of snow-clearing. Thereafter, progress was made without a hitch. Men worked silently and a way was cut through the drifts. At one point they left the road through a widened gateway and cut across open fields.

Astonishingly, only three hours after leaving Whitby, the *Robert Whitworth* was at the top of Bay Bank. The road down the village is so steep that for a distance the footpath alongside is a series of steps. That day, it was also ice-bound. The horses could not help, and were unyoked. Men took their places between the shafts, and ropes were attached to the carriage. By strength of their limbs, men acted as brakes to prevent the boat running away and being smashed. Steadily it was lowered and carefully manoeuvred round the sharp bend at the Laurel Inn. Its arrival on the beach was greeted by rousing cheers. Back in Whitby there was equal excitement, for notices displayed in the window of the offices of the *Whitby Gazette* enabled anxious townsfolk to follow the progress of the boat.

Between the wars, William Groves Barker, then the editor of the *Whitby Gazette*, broadcast an account of this journey on the BBC, and introduced Walter Currie, an old lifeboatman then in his seventy-third year, who had taken part in the momentous events of January 1881. The veteran, who

The Pull *by John Freeman. The Whitby lifeboat* Robert Whitworth *is pulled through Hawkser to the rescue at Robin Hoods Bay of the brig* Visitor *in January 1881.*

The Lifeboat Launch, *a watercolour by F H Mason depicting the final stages of the dramatic rescue of January 1881.*

had been a friend of Freeman, and shared ownership of a coble with him, enthusiastically recalled those cheers, and said that some of the drifts they encountered had been seven to eight feet (2-2.4m) in depth, and it was obstructions on this scale near Hawsker that caused them to take to the fields, which had partly been blown clear by the wind. He remembered, too, their anxiety as the boat was edged down Bay Bank.

The lifeboatmen had not stinted themselves during the journey, but their real task was to come. The *Robert Whitworth* was got into the water, and fatigue and aching limbs were either forgotten or ignored as they bent to their oars. Out into the raging gale they rowed, and it must have seemed to the crowds watching anxiously from the shore that the odds against them were too great.

For fully an hour they struggled, and were nearly swamped on several occasions. Then came a wave which snapped six oars, breaking them 'like so many straws', according to an eye-witness, and disabling the boat. Only by Henry Freeman's skill did the *Robert Whitworth* regain the shore. As some crewmen were exhausted and had to be replaced, a call was made for volunteers, and from the throng that stepped forward, Freeman chose one Bay man, John Skelton, who was able to direct the steersman through the tumbling water on the scaur. The vacant thwarts were manned by other volunteers, the broken oars replaced and partly double-banked — that is, two men to an oar — and, after three-quarters of an hour of hard rowing, Freeman put the lifeboat alongside the *Visitor*'s long-boat. Some of its occupants were unable even to speak following a seven-hour ordeal. Their deliverance was signalled by cheers from the lifeboat crew as they pulled alongside, and when the news spread that the *Visitor*'s men were safe, there was jubilation ashore, especially among the relatives of the three who lived in Bay, William Todd Anderson, the master, William Bell, the mate, and Jim Storm, a seaman. Mrs Anderson, the master's wife, had spent the day helped by neighbours in calm preparation for the safe return of her husband and his shipmates, confiding that, if she kept busy, she would have less time for worry. William Barker said in his radio broadcast:

> The enthusiasm when they were taken ashore was almost beyond description, and the lifeboat crew was entertained right royally by the Robin Hoods Bay folk, whose gratification was not lessened by their full knowledge of the difficulties and dangers which had been faced and overcome in the work of rescue.

In case the right royal entertainment is misinterpreted, the principal sustenance was derived from the Robin Hoods Bay Congregational Church bazaar, which happened to be taking place that day, although the Bay Hotel and the Laurel Inn probably had roles to play as well. A few days later, when the crew returned to Robin Hoods Bay, probably by rail, to collect the boat, the Rev Cooper arranged a service of thanksgiving, and then entertained the Whitby men to dinner at the Belle Hotel.

Rock of Ages

Henry Freeman's eminence in the local community was considered sufficient to earn him a picture-feature in the *Whitby Gazette* — a rare honour in those days — when he retired. Apart from his heroics as a lifeboatman, he had consistently demonstrated the knack of being in the right place at the right time when it came to life-saving.

In 1882, for example, he was returning in his coble from a fishing expedition when he saw a young swimmer in difficulty. With what a contemporary report described as 'great promptitude', he rowed to the scene, where a member of his crew dived over the side and brought the boy, who had already gone down for a third time, to the surface. The lad, who turned out to be the son of a Whitby hotelier, made a good recovery.

The picture of Freeman which accompanied the special supplement of the Whitby Gazette *to mark his retirement in October 1899.*

Seven years later, on a June day in 1889, he had taken a party to sea, and was putting his passengers ashore at Colliers Ghaut when a young woman missed her footing and fell headlong into the harbour. She could not have chosen a safer place for a ducking. Whitby's famous lifeboat coxswain promptly plucked her from the water. Suffering from nothing worse than a soaking, she was taken to the Talbot Hotel.

Then, on a summer day in 1898, Freeman and two companions were salmon-fishing when they saw that a boatman, Thomas Welham, had swum out from the beach in an attempt to save a holidaymaker who was in

A disabled barque off Whitby. (Whitby Literary & Philosophical Society.)

trouble in a choppy sea. Welham had a grip on the holidaymaker by the time Freeman brought the fishing coble alongside, but when the two men were dragged into the boat, it was found that the bather had perished.

His cobles were Freeman's special pride. He had one built by George Pearson of Spital Bridge, Whitby, which, according to the *Gazette,* was of 'superior model and design'. He had it launched by the wife of the Whitby Member of Parliament, and named it after her, *Louie Beckett.*

Freeman had his flaws. Mr Schill and Mr Minter, in their biography *Storm Warrior,* deal frankly with the humiliation he suffered in 1883 when Whitby magistrates convicted him of stealing lines from a fellow fisherman, which was bad enough, but he also had to suffer pontification against him in a leading article in the *Whitby Tmes.* The fact that he survived this as lifeboat coxswain and with his reputation intact is perhaps one of the more

Portrait of Henry Freeman. (Whitby Literary & Philosophical Society.)

remarkable tributes to Henry Freeman. There is, for example, no hint of anything short of adulation in a profile of *Heroes of the Whitby Lifeboat* published by W B Pickering:

> He is a splendid type of humanity with bronzed and intelligent face, and a broad chest which is adorned by the medal awarded to him for loyal service and heroism when the lifeboat has been forth to duty.

His lifeboat career ended in 1899, when he retired on a Lifeboat Institution pension of £12 per annum. During his last decade of service, he led forays into the West Riding to help RNLI fundraising, and appeared at Lifeboat Saturdays at Leeds, Halifax and Harrogate. A photo, apparently

Whitby lifeboatmen, prepared for a Lifeboat Saturday procession, pose in 1893 on what are believed to be the steps of Leeds Town Hall. Front row, from left to right: Thomas McGarry Kelly, Robert Richardson, Robert Eglon, Henry Freeman, Thomas Langlands, James Elder. Back row, left to right: William Harrison, Edward Gash, Joseph Tomlinson, William Affleck, Pounder Robinson, Walter Corrie. (Dora M Walker's Freemen of the Sea.*)*

taken on the steps of Leeds Town Hall, shows Freeman and his crewmen posing somewhat uneasily in caps, and wearing cork lifejackets of the kind which saved his life in 1861.

Had he been able to read, he would have enjoyed *Between the Heather and the Northern Sea* by the Whitby novelist Mary Linskill, which included a vivid account of the *Visitor* rescue, in which names were changed, but which in most respects stuck pretty close to the facts. Mary Linksill wrote of the rescue: '... the day and the deed will live, as brave deeds have lived in England always'. Her book was first published in 1884, and went through six reprints. It was still in demand in 1903, when Macmillans brought it out in its popular Sixpenny series.

Freeman died at his cottage in Bakehouse Yard, which slopes steeply down from Cliff Street to Haggersgate and thence the harbourside. In attendance was the Rev E W Challenger, who was later to conduct his funeral, and confide that the great man, though semi-conscious, had been able to follow the words of the hymn *Rock of Ages* which, he said, were the last words Henry Freeman was to utter.

He had no children. His first marriage, to Elizabeth Busfield, whose father was a jet ornament manufacturer, was celebrated in 1861. She died in 1898 and three years later, in defiance of the Table of Kindred and Affinity and the law of the land, as it then was, he married her sister Emma, a widow who had three children with her first husband. Henry had a number of nephews and nieces, including one of special interest to the writer. She was Alice Freeman, the illegitimate daughter of Henry's eldest sister, Ann, who was born at Bridlington in 1852. Aged eighteen, and living in Bagdale, Whitby, having migrated to the town like other members of the family, she married Thomas Hunter, a jet manufacturer with an address in Baxtergate, at the Parish Church of St Mary's on Christmas Day, 1870. Their first child was Emily, my paternal grandmother. Thus, Henry Freeman's father was my great-great-great-grandfather — tenuous, perhaps, but satisfying nonetheless. Alice Hunter seemed to have remained close to her uncle, and was a leading mourner at his funeral.

He went to his grave on the shoulders of lifeboatmen in a coffin draped with the Union flag, and was much mourned. A Mr George Whittick of Liverpool was moved to verse, which was published in the *Whitby Gazette*:

> Though Britain has many a boatman
> As brave as our hero dead,
> Yet the memory of Henry Freeman
> With Whitby's fame will be wed.

There is a lot of truth in that. Henry Freeman may owe his posthumous familiarity to images captured by Frank Meadow Sutcliffe, but he more than earned his fame during those gallant years when he frequently pitted his own life against the elements to save the lives of others. Surely nobody has a better right to epitomise those heroes of the sea, the Victorian rowing lifeboatmen.